Survival Audit & Calculations Manual

JOSEPH BOUNDS

Copyright © 2014 Joseph Bounds

All rights reserved.

ISBN: 1505425573

INTRODUCTION

I request people using this manual do not make copies for others and do not otherwise distribute these materials as they are copyrighted under the laws of the United States of America and intended only for those individuals or groups that purchased this manual. Presumably you paid for this manual and others should also pay their fair share. If you do make or receive copies of these materials without purchasing them, then consider these materials stolen.

I have no doubt there are people who will disagree with some of the numerical values that are part of this audit. That is fine, but the important principles do not change. If you do not like the numbers – want more ammo, or whatever – just change them and continue your audit to see how your current preparations measure up with how you want to be. The purpose is to cover important areas and once this is done you and / or your group will be better off in determining how you stand.

This audit is the result of being a lifelong prepper and watching out for events that place everyday existence in jeopardy. The audit is therefore in part the result of personal experience, military training as a nuclear fallout shelter commander in the cold war, research into group behavior, and practical survival requirements. It presents my professional opinion on major requirements while setting realistic stocking levels. Covering all possible minutia is not possible or attempted because in many cases these represent personal opinions and beliefs of the individual that span a very broad range of subjects.

The Survival Audit & Calculations Manual is intended to assess an individual's or group's preparations to meet demands occurring in a long-term survival situation in lieu of having a consultant evaluation. While no method can address every possible facet of survival due to the dynamic, changing environment, and various individual factors, it addresses many preparation areas not normally covered in the popular public media to provide a more complete readiness assessment. No practical method can assess an individual's or group's determination, innovation, or resourcefulness until put to an actual test.

This manual addresses 19 primary and 15 sustainability areas in meeting long-term survival challenges. Detailed instructions allow completing each section to rate current performance and to point out possible improvements.

Nothing can prepare an individual or group against the unforeseen or rogue actions of an individual or hostile group. Vigilance, attention to detail, and maintaining a low profile reduces risk of exposure and in my opinion is the best form of passive defense. Effective communication monitoring within the local community as well as state, and federal government about events and actions of individuals and groups can aid in preparing for events leading up to a survival situation as well as for contingencies after it happens. It is the hope that this manual will better ready an individual or group for a long-term survival event when it occurs. May the odds be in your favor and Murphy's Law on your side as you prepare for uncertainties waiting in the future. I support the Second Amendment to the United States Constitution and if you hold spiritual values, may God bless and keep you safe in uncertain times.

- Joseph Bounds

CONTENTS

- SPECIALIZED SURVIVAL SCENARIOS 1
  - Nuclear 1
  - Biological 2
  - Chemical 3
- PEOPLE 4
- WATER RESERVES 8
  - Water Sustainability 9
- FOOD RESERVES 10
  - Food Sustainability 12
- COMMUNICATIONS 13
  - Communications Sustainability 14
- SECURITY RESOURCES 15
  - Defense and Assault Rifles 15
  - Defense and Assault Rifle Sustainability 17
  - Hunting / Sniping Rifles 17
  - Hunting / Sniping Sustainability 18
  - Defensive Handguns 19
  - Handgun Sustainability 20
  - Defensive / Hunting Shotguns 21
  - Shotgun Sustainability 22
  - Small Game / Varmint Weapons 22
  - Small Game / Pest Control Sustainability 23
- AMMUNITION RELOADING 24
- SHELTER RESOURCES 26
  - Shelter Sustainability 27
- SAFETY / FIRST AID / MEDICAL 28
- TRANSPORTATION RESOURCES 30
  - Transportation Sustainability 31
- LEADERSHIP 33
  - Leadership Sustainability 34
- SKILLS TO TRADE 36

- UNIQUE FACTORS 38
  - Unique Factors Sustainability 38
- CLOTHING AND PERSONAL PROTECTIVE EQUIPMENT 40
- HYGIENE MAINTENANCE 42
  - Hygiene Maintenance Sustainability 43
- SHELTER MAINTENANCE 44
  - Shelter Maintenance Sustainability 44
- AUXILIARY EQUIPMENT 46
  - Auxiliary Equipment Sustainability 47
- ABILITY TO TRAIN / EDUCATE OTHER PEOPLE 48
- WORSHIP / SPIRITUAL 50
- Summary 51
- ABOUT THE AUTHOR 52

ACKNOWLEDGMENTS

I would be remiss in my acknowledgments if not recognizing God and His help through all the events of my life. He has endowed me with skills in structured thinking, organization, intelligence, and many others. My life experiences are the result of His guidance and my stumbling. The true survivors and preppers are those people who prepare, but keep a low profile so as to make a lesser target of themselves and resources. There will be those who will try to take what you have – feel they are somehow more entitled, whether survivor or other preppers – BE WARNED!

SPECIALIZED SURVIVAL SCENARIOS

There are many potential long-term survival scenarios and it is not possible to address the specifics of every conceivable possibility, therefore three specialized scenarios follow. If living in a metropolitan area, the possibility of some event is greater, though small, than living in a more rural setting. Terrorists want bang for the buck as well as publicity and therefore are not likely to slip a nuke into famer Brown's barn, attempt an Ebola pandemic in the middle of Nebraska wheat fields, or a chemical attack in the outback of nowhere. However, there are basics that should be observed if an incident occurs or there is belief some type of event could occur for whatever reason where you reside.

Nuclear

A nuclear scenario may occur under several possibilities that include, but are not limited to an accident at a power generation station, terrorist action, and limited to full scale nuclear war. There may be little or no time of such an event ahead of time. The following table lists some basic preparations specific to this type of incident.

Specialized – Nuclear		
		Points
1	Ability to monitor emergency broadcasts – radio, television, etc.	
2	Ability to leave an area by motorized transportation or on foot	
3	3 day bug out bag prepared for each person's immediate relocation	
4	Ability to seal doors and windows if advised to do so	
5	Radiation meter for monitoring exposure	
6	Ability to calculate radiation exposure levels of people	
7	Ability to decontaminate people and clothing as needed	
8	Specialized training for dealing with a nuclear event	
9	Shelter area prepared to deal with this event	
	Total:	
	Max Total:	

Important to remember when preparing for a nuclear event are the three factors of time, distance, and shielding. It is important to note that the table items are basic preparations and detailed planning and preparations need learning from and coordination with knowledgeable individuals. Seek out such individuals, agencies, and do your own research in preparation to meet specific requirements.

Score 2 points for each item in the table and zero if not prepared. As Nuclear is covered as a specialized scenario and open to many more items, the points score is not specific in the summary table at the end. Please note that the detailed preparation of a 3-day bug out bag is not included. There are many sources and opinions on what is needed to complete this type of resource. Consult several sources and modify the requirements based on an evaluation of your particular needs.

Biological

Biological agents tend to be local in their effectiveness. Exceptions to this rule are agents whose purpose would be to cause an epidemic or pandemic of some disease. Distance and isolation from the area and individuals affected are some common methods of isolating transmission.

	Specialized – Biological	
		Points
1	Ability to monitor emergency broadcasts – radio, television, etc.	
2	Ability to leave an area by motorized transportation or on foot	
3	3 day bug out bag prepared for each person's immediate relocation	
4	Ability to seal doors and windows if advised to do so	
5	Ability to decontaminate people and clothing as needed	
6	Specialized training for dealing with a biological event	
7	Shelter area prepared to deal with this event	
	Total:	
	Max Total:	

It is important to note the table items are basic preparations and detailed planning and preparations need training and coordination with knowledgeable individuals. Seek out such individuals, agencies, and do your own research in preparation to meet specific requirements.

Score 2 points for each item in the table and zero if not prepared. As Biological is covered as a specialized scenario and open to many more items, the points score is not specific in the summary table at the end. Please note that the detailed preparation of a 3-day bug out bag is not included. There are many sources and opinions on what is needed to complete this type of resource preparation. Consult several sources and modify the requirements based on an evaluation of your particular needs.

Chemical

Chemical agents are affected by time, distance, and weather to name a few factors. When dispensed for use in the atmosphere, they are subject to wind direction in determining their effect.

Specialized – Chemical		
		Points
1	Ability to monitor emergency broadcasts – radio, television, etc.	
2	Ability to leave an area by motorized transportation or on foot	
3	3 day bug out bag prepared for each person's immediate relocation	
4	Ability to seal doors and windows if advised to do so	
5	Ability to decontaminate people and clothing as needed	
6	Specialized training fpr dealing with a chemical event	
7	Shelter area prepared to deal with this event	
	Total:	
	Max Total:	

Score 2 points for each item in the table and zero if not prepared. As Chemical is covered as a specialized scenario and open to many more items, As Nuclear is covered as a specialized scenario and open to many more items, As Nuclear is covered as a specialized scenario and open to many more items, the points score is not specific in the summary table at the end. Please note that the detailed preparation of a 3-day bug out bag is not included. There are many sources and opinions on what is needed to complete this type of resource preparation. Consult several sources and modify the requirements based on an evaluation of your particular needs.

PEOPLE

There are several factors to consider for the parameters defining the number of people. What is a minimum effective size? What is a maximum effective size? What are the needs in relation to the four major requirements of survival for the long-term? What are the logistic considerations in terms of size and various other areas of support needed? How do children factor into group dynamics? What are the sustainability requirements of groups of various sizes? Let us now consider these issues in light of long-term individual group survival.

What is the minimum effective group size? Minimum effective group size is 4 adults. This is because a division of labor is a definite asset in long-term survival. There is a need to stand guard over the group and to alert its members in case of approaching danger, to watch over its material resources and shelter area on a 24-hour a day, 7 day a week basis. During this time other activities need to take place that support the group through meals, possible foraging for replacement stocks, and eventually crop planting and harvesting. Breaking the group into 2 people to stand watch puts them on a 12-hour shift, 8 hours if shared between 3 people and 6 hours if all share in the security responsibilities.

With 4 people there are 96 man-hours each day (24 x 4). One quarter of this is required if only one person at a time is on guard duty, but this spreads the ability of a single individual thin when responsible for 360-degrees around a location. However it is arranged, a given number of man-hours must be consumed to support security and another amount of hours consumed for sleeping. This leaves each person the remaining hours each day to take care of and accomplish the many other requirements of daily living. Long-term survival is a challenging scenario at best and meeting these challenges becomes an even more daunting task if the group size is smaller or if children are part of the matrix. When the group size shrinks to 1 or 2 adults, the risks become greater as one or two people cannot perform all necessary tasks and face the challenges of seasonal environmental changes.

What about the other end of the spectrum, maximum group size? Maximum group size for this discussion is 16 adults. This is due to personal experience leading six sigma teams for improvement projects and research into what constitutes a maximum effective group size. In many instances leaders fail to effectively control groups beyond 8 to 10 members, while others can maintain effectiveness with a few more members. The number is set at 16 to grant the benefit of a doubt, however, fewer members are preferred.

Reasons for limiting group size are several. All areas of support and maintenance increase dramatically to include shelter area, food, water, security, and so forth as a group's size grows. Increased size does improve security because individuals or smaller groups are not as likely to attack a larger, well-armed, and organized group. As mentioned above, size has its detriments to include people who tend to just go through the motions without effectively contributing to daily maintenance and group survival – in short they are along for the ride and consuming valuable resources. It is the leader's job to evaluate how every individual is contributing to the group's well-being. To be blunt, if there are such individuals, they need to be given productive tasks and if all they want to do is bitch and complain it is best they find their own way. If necessary to remove disruptive individuals from the group, it is important to take measures to revise implemented security measures to prevent the possibility they may be able to compromise the group's well-being through intentional or unintentional actions.

There needs to be a balance between adult males and adult females in the group to prevent rivalries and distractions from occurring in the high stress environment created in long-term survival. While this may not be possible, there are some points awarded when this is not a perfect balance. With proper screening and evaluation, additional members may be added after the event happens, but be alert to possible security concerns when doing this.

Children are also a factor in daily survival requirements as their needs must be addressed as well as security, entertainment, any special requirements, and ages. Individual maturity levels need consideration and generally, to set a cutoff, children age 12 and older are thought to be able to contribute at least in a minor way to daily operations such as preparing food, gathering fire wood, caring for animals, harvesting, and so on as their abilities and skills permit. For these reasons additional credit is permitted if there are children age 12 and older.

Provisions need to be made in caring for younger children and their needs. Children place additional support and security requirements on the group in the immediate and long-term for group sustainability. Training them on what to do for specific events is needed.

All work and no play, or other methods of relieving stress, is a bad combination in the long-term for adults and children. There is a need for games, entertainment, and other distractions to provide an outlet for these forces. Staying on high alert for long periods of time is not healthy and can contribute to health disorders related to stress.

The maximum score for the people that comprise your group is 20. If your score is less, there is possibly a need to re-evaluate these factors. These are not the only people factors taken into consideration and others are evaluated in additional sections.

	People			
		Number		Points
1	Total Number of Adults		Group Size:	
2	Number of Adult Males		Male Balance:	
3	Number of Adult Females		Female Balance:	
4	Number of Children		Number of children 12 and older:	
5	Is there a pre-arranged schedule for child care rotation? Enter Yes or No			
6	Has various types of entertainment been established for adults and children? Enter Yes or No			
			Total:	
			Max Total:	

SURVIVAL AUDIT & CALCULATIONS

Instructions for People

1. Under Number, enter total number of adults for item 1
2. Under Number, enter the number of adult males in the group for item 2
3. Under Number, enter the number of adult females in the group for item 3
4. Under Number, enter the number of children in the group for item 4
5. Under Number, enter Yes or No if there is a prearranged schedule for child care rotation
6. Under Number, enter Yes or No if different types of entertainment has been established for adults and children.
7. Under Points, Group Size, enter 4 if group size is 4 to 16 adults. If less than 4 or greater than 16 enter a 2.
8. Under Points, Male Balance, enter 4 if the number of adult males is equal to the number of adult females. If the number of adult males is more than adult females, enter 2.
9. Under Points, Female Balance, enter 4 if the number of adult females is equal to the number of adult males. If the number of adult females is more than adult males, enter 2.
10. Under Points, Number of children 12 and older, if there are any children age 12 and older enter 2, otherwise enter 0.
11. If there is a prearranged child care rotation schedule, under Points enter 4.
12. If there are prearranged entertainment methods established, under Points enter 2.
13. Total points and compare to maximum available points of 20.

Notes:

WATER RESERVES

Water reserve is a major category of long-term survival. Some survival sources expect a year or more of water to be supplied for each member of a group. However, in many cases this is not practical in space required, additional monetary cost, or viable long-term product reliability. Situations indicate that as and after a scenario unfolds, a 90 day supply is an adequate initial on-hand stock. Failure of a relied upon source, such as a municipal water distribution system can create problems in the long-term. However, additional points are allocated for one or more resupply sources such as a creek, river, or lake nearby.

If the resupply source is some distance away, there is a de-rating factor applied due to greater exposure risk. There are additional points for optional methods of water transportation, windmills, and gravity fed systems as well as methods of filtering, removing contaminants, and chemical processing.

	Water Reserves			
		Number		Points
1	Number of Gallons Stored			
2	Number of Gallons Needed			
	Sustainability			
3	Water Resupply Source 1		De-rating Factor:	
4	Water Resupply Source 2		De-rating Factor:	
5	Off Grid Water Transport 1, Yes or No			
6	Off Grid Water Transport 2, Yes or No			
7	Capacity to Boil Water, Yes or No			
8	Capacity to Filter Water, Yes or No			
9	Capacity to Chemically Treat Water			
			Total:	
			Max Total:	32

SURVIVAL AUDIT & CALCULATIONS

The first requirement is for a 90 day water storage to supply each group member with a minimum of 1 gallon per day consumption. Proceed as follows:

1. Under Number, enter the number of gallons currently stored in item 1
2. Under Number, multiply the total number of people in the group by 90 and enter in item 2. If the amount entered in 1 is greater than or equal to the amount entered in 2, enter 4 points. If the amount entered in 1 greater than or equal to half of that entered in 2, enter 2 points, otherwise enter zero.

Water Sustainability

3. Under Number, for each available resupply source in items 3 & 4 enter a four, "4". De-rating factors: If a resupply source is more than 200 yards from the shelter structure, enter 0.5 and multiply to get allowed points, if a resupply source is closer than 200 yards enter a one, "1" as a de-rating factor.
4. Under Number for 5 & 6, for each available alternate transport method, such as a tanker trailer, enter four, "4"
5. Under Number, for capacity to boil, filter, and chemically purify water in items 7, 8, & 9 enter a four, "4", if there are applicable resources to perform these functions.

There are 32 total possible points for the Water Reserve category. A lower score indicates the possibility of a need to evaluate scores on elements contained in this section.

Notes:

FOOD RESERVES

Food reserve is a major category in long-term survival. Though not as time critical to the human body as water reserve, an individual or group cannot hope to last nine months or longer without an initial food reserve and an ability to restock or grow additional sustenance. While water is replenished in nature, there cannot be hope that edible materials will restock quickly. Expect supplies to be quickly taken from commercial sources. Also, there is a high probability there will be many refugees in your area with all types of guns, other weapons, and they will be decimating available wildlife as they flee immediate peril. For these reasons, do not expect to restock your food reserves through hunting, etc. in the near future.

Count on people trying to take what you have as the crisis becomes worse over time and starvation approaches. This situation will require maintaining safety in numbers and a high degree of alertness when venturing from the relative safety of your shelter. Share what you possibly can through a local church or other organization, but one cannot hope to feed hundreds or possibly thousands of refugees in your local area without reducing your own survival chances.

Another factor to be aware of is that local authorities or self appointed "regulatory groups" may try to confiscate your supplies in the name of the greater good through "official" actions that attempt to give their organization some level of legitimacy. The question here becomes, how high is their resolve in taking what you have and how high is your resolve in preventing it?

Redundancy is a key element in maintaining a food reserve and contributes to sustaining the group. It is possible that you have built one or more resupply sources such as a large chicken coup, hydroponics garden, small cattle herd, etc. and these aid survival through renewable food stocks and add additional points to the overall calculations. One or more ways to preserve food, seed stored for future crops, and members possessing experience in hunting, fishing, trapping, and so forth contribute to redundant food reserve methods.

Because of the potential difficulty in restocking food in the immediate and possibly the long-term, a 270-day supply for each person is required. This is calculated at a caloric requirement of 2,200 calories per day as there is likely to be little sleep and long hours under varying levels of moderate to high stress combined with increased physical activity.

Having one or more methods to preserve food creates a redundancy for food storage. These methods may include canning, freezing, smoking, drying, and so forth and add points to maintaining a viable food supply. Seeds stored for future crops also add points to maintaining food supplies. Though in the short-term an ability to hunt and fish may be limited, over time the wildlife populations can be expected to renew themselves and these will contribute to sustainable food supplies in the long term.

Provision should be made to store food materials for any livestock, pets, and security animals. There are no points allocated for these in the chart as these vary by circumstance. It may be very difficult to obtain feed for these items in the short term. Point scoring follows.

* Please note these requirements do not take into account special dietary needs or a need to maintain a balanced diet.

	Food Reserves			
		Number		Points
1	Number of calories stored			
2	Number of calories needed			
	Sustainability			
3	First resupply source			
4	Second resupply source			
5	First preservation method			
6	Second preservation method			
7	Seeds stored for crops			
8	Ability to hunt, trap, fish, etc.			
			Total:	
			Max Total:	34

1. Under Number for item 1, most prepackaged foodstuffs indicate the number of servings and calories. Count the number of calories in your food storage and enter this total.

2. Under Number for item 2, multiply the number of people (adults and children) in your group by 594,000 to obtain a total calorie requirement for your group and enter this total. Example: 6 people x 594,000 = 3,564,000 total calories.

3. Under Number if line 1 is greater than or equal to line 2 enter ten, "10", points under Points for line 2. If line 1 is less than item 2, divide item 1 by item 2 and multiply by 10 to obtain the value to place under item 2 Points.

Food Sustainability

4. Under Number for line 3 and 4, if you have one or more resupply sources as discussed above, enter 4 points on the lines for item 3 and / or item 4.

5. Under Number for line 5 and 6, preservation methods such as canning, smoking, drying, and so on adds to sustainability of food stocks without wasting valuable material. Add 4 points for each method possessed in items 5 and / or 6.

6. Under Number for line 7, if you have stored seed for various crops, add four, "4", points for item 7.

7. Under Number for line 8, if members of your group have skills in hunting, fishing, or gathering wild foods add four, "4", points for item 8.

There are 34 possible points for the Food Reserve category. Scoring is less may indicate areas where you want to improve by reviewing your point scores in each area.

Notes:

COMMUNICATIONS

Communications can be an important area in the overall survival scenario, but is not one of the four major categories. The ability to coordinate activities, alert people to threats and monitor what is taking place in the outside environment of local government, police actions, and emergency response provide valuable information while preventing the group from feeling totally isolated in stressful times. Two-way communications also provides the ability to stay in contact with other groups and if need be, coordinate support activities. Especially in the early days and weeks it will be important to have someone monitoring broadcasts 24-hours a day to stay up to date on external activities taking place.

	Communications	
		Points
1	Base radios available	
2	Vehicle radios available	
3	Personal radios available	
4	Emergency / commercial radios available	
	Sustainability	
5	Spare radios available	
6	Spare batteries available	
7	Backup power supply available	
	Total:	
	Max Total:	14

1. Under Points, enter two, "2", points for base radios that can monitor your mobile radios (personal and vehicular) as well as local, state, and federal broadcasts.

2. Under Points, enter two, "2", points if there are radios for transmitting and receiving information in one or more vehicles.

3. Under Points, enter two, "2", points if there are personal radios that can be carried by individuals for communication with vehicles and the base stations.

4. Under Points, enter two, "2", points if there are radios for monitoring emergency and commercial station broadcasts.

Communications Sustainability

5. Under Points, enter two, "2", points if there are spare radios to replace base, vehicular, and personal radios should they become, lost, damaged, etc.

6. Under Points, enter two, "2", points for space batteries and backup power sources to maintain communications and / or charge batteries for communication equipment.

7. Under Points, total your score, 14 points available, evaluate areas if changes are needed.

Notes:

SECURITY RESOURCES

Security Resources is an important element in the overall long-term survival scenario and is one of four major categories. It is reasonable to assume individuals who find themselves without needed resources for an extended survival event will try to take whatever possible from other individuals and groups. They may be armed with a variety of weapons varying from rifles, shotguns, pistols, hunting bows, and whatever other improvised weapons they have acquired. Therefore it is important to provide weapons for your and the group's long term security. If you are part of a group, different individuals can contribute a range of weapons and ammunition without one single person needing to face the acquisition cost and storage requirements. An added advantage is that different people get to bring various weapon types to the party. It becomes more difficult for one or two individuals, especially if eventually forced to bug out, to take a large range of weapons with them if on foot, but more practical if relocating by vehicle between sites is possible. Be selective in your weapons choice so they can be versatile in playing more than one role.

Security Resources is broken into five areas of concentration: Defense and Assault rifles, Hunting and Sniping rifles, Defensive Handguns, Defense and Hunting Shotguns, and Small Game and Pest Control weapons. Ammunition requirements may seem high, but remember this has to last 270 days (9 months) and possibly longer. The reason for different magazine requirements in the categories is the role they play and the same for ammunition requirements. It is expected that people will be trained in marksmanship, selective in their targets, and not firing wildly.

Defense and Assault Rifles

Some weapons may fall into more than one category, do not list more than once because loss of a weapon through damage, malfunction, and so forth will impact multiple areas. List each individual weapon by caliber. List the number of magazines available for each weapon. List the number of different types of rounds available for each weapon.

Security Resources – Defense / Assault Rifles								
Caliber	Magazines	Ammo Count	Ammo Count	Ammo Count	Mag Points	Ammo Points	Weapon Points	Total
								Commonality:
								Total:
								Possible Points

Rifles

If there are at least ½ as many rifles as adults, example (12 adults x ½ = 6) enter 4 points per rifle, less than ½ as many rifles as adults, score 2 points each. The maximum effective group size is 16. Therefore, only 8 lines are included in the table to meet minimum requirements. Because this classification focuses on defense and assault type weapons, there is a need for semiautomatic and automatic style weapons, if magazines are not applicable to a particular rifle entered into this category score 2 points for the weapon.

Magazines

Score 4 points if there are 5 or more magazines for a rifle (20 – 30 rds. each). If there are two or more magazines score 2 points, less than 2 magazines score zero, "0". If part of a group of four adults with each firing five magazines of 30 rounds is 600 rounds expended – a lot of shooting. Be selective and let the enemy waist their valuable resources.

Ammunition

Different types of ammunition are allowed with three columns for different ammo types.

If there are more than three types combine them into the available space. If there are a minimum of 500 or more total rounds for a single rifle score 4 points. If there is at least 250 rounds, but less than 500 rounds score 2 points. Less than 250 rounds for a rifle scores zero, "0" points. Five hundred rounds is a <u>minimum</u> established in case a physical relocation on foot is required and permits taking most if not all ammunition with you.

Defense and Assault Rifle Sustainability

If there are two or more rifles of the same caliber, add 2 points for each rifle of the same caliber, example you have two .223 rifles and four .308 rifles, and one .45 machine gun = (2 + 2) + (4 x 2) = 12 additional Commonality points. This permits continued use of ammunition if there is a loss of a weapon for any reason.

Total possible points are number of rifles x 12, example 7 rifles x 12 = 84, plus commonality points 12 = 96. The machine gun cannot be counted as having a like caliber for an additional 2 points because there is only one weapon available in .45 caliber. There are potentially 112 possible points, adjust as necessary for your group size.

Hunting / Sniping Rifles

This category is different from Defense and Assault Rifles. These weapons are more likely to be utilized at greater ranges to obtain large game such as deer and to eliminate dangerous targets. The support requirements for these weapons differ because smaller quantities of ammunition are likely to be circulated through them. Target practice or qualification exercises are not likely to take place because these would drain valuable, scarce resources. It is a good idea to maintain common calibers with the Defense and Assault Rifle group to avoid stocking calibers that may be difficult to find in a post survival event world.

Rifles

If there are at least ½ as many rifles as adults, example (12 adults x ½ = 6), score 4 points per rifle, less than ½ as many rifles as adults, score 2 points each. The maximum

Security Resources – Hunting / Sniping Rifles								
Caliber	Magazines	Ammo Count	Ammo Count	Ammo Count	Mag Points	Ammo Points	Weapon Points	Total
							Commonality:	
							Total:	
							Possible Points	

effective group size is 16. Therefore, only 8 lines are included in the table to meet minimum requirements. Precise target selection and takedown are key in maintaining resources.

Magazines

There may or may not be detachable magazines for rifles in this category due to the fact that assault weapons tend to be semiautomatic or automatic and these rifles may have internal magazines and bolt actions. Score 4 points if there are 2 or more detachable magazines or if there is only an internal magazine. If a rifle has magazines, score 2 points if there are less than two magazines.

Ammunition

Different types of ammunition are allowed with three columns for different ammo types. If there are a <u>minimum</u> of 250 or more rounds for a single rifle score 4 points. If there is at least 150 rounds, but less than 250 rounds score 2 points. Less than 250 rounds for a rifle scores zero, "0" points.

Hunting / Sniping Sustainability

If there are two or more rifles of the same caliber, add 2 points for each rifle of the same caliber, example you have two 30-06 rifles, three .308 rifles, and one .270 rifle = (2 + 2)

+ (3 x 2) = 10 additional commonality points. This permits continued use of ammunition if there is a loss of one weapon for any reason.

Total possible points are number of rifles x 12, example 6 rifles x 12 = 72, plus commonality points 10 = 82. The .270 cannot be counted as a common caliber for an additional 2 points because there is only one weapon available in this caliber. There are potentially 112 possible points, adjust as needed for your group's size.

Defensive Handguns

It is possible that everyone will need to be armed at one time or another. This may be during a time the survival complex is under attack or people are outside performing regular duties and need to be armed for an unexpected event. In a situation where there are possibly gangs, semi organized groups, or just rogue individuals and animals, armed is good sense.

Defensive Resources – Handguns								
Caliber	Magazines	Ammo Count	Ammo Count	Ammo Count	Mag Points	Ammo Points	Weapon Points	Total
							Commonality:	
							Total:	
							Possible Points	

One can also expect in a long-term survival situation for people to turn their pets (especially dogs) loose to fend for themselves. Dogs are pack hunters and may roam from one area to another and create a hazard to livestock and people. Cats can become wild and decimate the local game bird, rabbit, and squirrel populations. There is also the possibility of these animals becoming rabid and presenting a serious health threat. Be wise, be armed when outside.

Handguns are short range weapons for when things go from bad to really ugly and there is a need for close, personal defense. The natural recommendation is to keep the number of calibers to a minimum – depending upon each individual's ability to control his or her weapon in a safe manner. It is also wise to obtain calibers commonly in use so stocking and restocking ammunition is not a problem. A weapon need not have a large capacity as long as an individual can accurately hit the target. Scoring is 4 points for each weapon with the requirement each adult have access to a handgun of their own, 14 adults = 14 pistols. Yours is the choice of weapon, caliber, and magazine capacity.

Magazines

Magazine requirement is 4 for each weapon to score 4 points, two or three magazines scores 2 points, if magazines are not applicable to the weapon enter N/A and score 2 points. Magazines hold various amounts of ammunition, with a capacity of 8 rounds per magazine this is an immediate 32 rounds available, 18 rounds is 72.

Ammunition

Ammunition is a <u>minimum</u> of 250 rounds for each weapon to score 4 points, 150 and above scores 2 points, and less than 150 rounds score zero points.

Handgun Sustainability

Redundancy in calibers is with two or more weapons of the same caliber, count an additional 2 points for each weapon. Calibers common with rifles and handguns are not considered redundant. There are potentially 224 possible points, adjust for your group size.

Defensive / Hunting Shotguns

A powerful defensive weapon, shotguns have few rivals at short range. They have the capacity to be chambered with different types of ammunition and have different barrel lengths for application against a variety of targets. Buckshot and rifled slugs are common rounds used for larger game and are effective against threatening targets. Smaller pellets, shot rounds, are good for hunting smaller game such as rabbits and squirrels.

Shotguns

Because of their versatility in hunting and defense, the requirement is for half as many shotguns as there are adults, 12 adults = 6 shotguns. Few shotguns have detachable magazines with the most common being tubular magazines. Score 4 points if the tube or magazine is capable of carrying 4 or more rounds plus one in the chamber.

Security Resources – Defensive / Hunting Shotguns								
Caliber	Magazines	Ammo Count	Ammo Count	Ammo Count	Mag Points	Ammo Points	Weapon Points	Total
							Commonality:	
							Total:	
							Possible Points	

Ammunition

Ammunition requirement is for a <u>minimum</u> of 250 rounds per shotgun to score 4 points and may be of a variety of slugs, buckshot, and shot sizes. More than 150 rounds scores 2 points, less than 150 rounds score zero.

Shotgun Sustainability

Score an additional 2 points for each shotgun that has another of the same gauge, example: 4-12ga pump action, 2-20ga semi-auto, 1-16ga pump = 4x2 + 2x2 = 12 additional points for same gauge. Total possible points are number of shotguns (8 x 12) + redundancy points (8 x 2) = 112 possible points, adjust as needed for your group size.

Small Game / Pest Control Weapons

Small Game and Varmint Weapons is a fairly open category depending upon how one wants to apply these weapons. Application may involve smaller gauge shotguns, the ever popular .22 rifle or pistol, bows and arrows, blow guns, sling shots, etc. Important is skillful application against their intended target.

Security Resources – Small Game / Pest Control								
Caliber	Magazines	Ammo Count	Ammo Count	Ammo Count	Mag Points	Ammo Points	Weapon Points	Total
								Commonality:
								Total:
								Possible Points

Though set up for rifles, count any weapon used against small game or varmints, but do not count them if used in a previous category. Redundancy is a valuable thing and having a weapon that can utilize common projectiles increases flexibility in deployment. Each weapon listed counts 4 points.

Magazines

Magazines count 4 points if there are 2 or more and 2 points for one. If the category is not applicable enter N/A and 4 points.

Ammunition

Because of the flexibility of this category, ammunition is counted at the rate of 500 rounds for weapons such as .22 rifle and pistols. If other weapons are used, such as a bow and arrows, it is up to the individual to determine what an adequate amount would be over the initial 270 day interval to score 4 points, 2 points if this amount is between half and the full amount, and zero if less than half. Remember, if you are out hunting small game or dispatching a pest, you may have to fight your way back to base if the unexpected occurs.

Small Game / Pest Control Sustainability

Total possible points are total number of weapons multiplied by 12. Redundancy counts if there are multiple weapons capable of utilizing the same ammunition type. There are potentially 112 possible points, adjust as needed for your group size.

Notes:

AMMUNITION RELOADING

This area is related to, but different from, having several rifles, pistols, or shotguns chambered for the same ammunition caliber. Reloading empty casings generates a new ammunition supply. Having common calibers (redundancy) reduces cost because there are fewer equipment dies to purchase and there may be cost discounts in buying larger quantities of primers, powder, and bullets. Personal experience reloading ammunition indicates that one powder sometimes can be used over a range of calibers and this simplifies and increases efficiency of the reloading process by having fewer items to change out when going from one caliber of rifle or handgun to another. The key is to do your research and determine which components to standardize on.

The components listed in the table below are a starting point to consider in reloading ammunition. If not familiar with reloading it is wise to consult people familiar with the

	Ammunition Reloading	
		Points
1	Reloading press for rifle and pistol cartridges	
2	Reloading dies for rifle and pistol cartridges	
3	Reloading press for shotgun shells	
4	Reloading dies for shotgun shells	
5	Primers for rifle cases	
6	Weighing scale	
7	Primers for pistol cases	
8	Primers for shotgun shells	
9	Bullets for rifle cases	
10	Bullets for pistol cases	
11	Loads (shot, buckshot, slugs) for shotgun shells	
12	Powder for rifle cartridges	
13	Powder for pistol cartridges	
14	Powder for shotgun shells	
15	Reloading manual	
	Total:	
	Max Total:	

operations involved to determine what specific equipment you want to use and they can also provide guidance on which reloading components will provide the greatest versatility for your particular weapon calibers. You may also want to purchase a good reloading manual to browse in making your final choices. Be aware that higher velocity (maximum or "hot") loads place greater stress on ammunition casings as well as the weapon and may result in reduced life cycles for both. The table below is not intended to be all inclusive, but creates as a starting point in setting up your ammunition redundancy process. More than one person should become familiar with reloading operations.

Enter 4 points for each item on the table. Maximum score is 60, but is not inclusive of all possible equipments and combinations, adjust scoring appropriately.

Notes:

SHELTER RESOURCES

Shelter resources evaluate the status of the shelter itself and physical capabilities. The first six items address the shelter's physical location along with other personnel protective factors associated with a physical structure. A closer proximity to a major population area increases the possibility that a shelter could come under attack from larger numbers of refugees fleeing the long-term survival event. As with other areas previously addressed, sustainability is an important factor in continued viability in a survival situation.

	Shelter Resources	Points
1	Proximity to a town of 50,000 or more, ____ miles / 60 = ____ x 4	
2	Property has an underground bunker, ____ yes, ____ no	
3	Property has a basement, ____ yes, ____ no	
4	Building has a safe room, ____ yes, ____ no	
5	There is a local sense of community, ____ yes, ____ no	
Sustainability		
6	Off Grid Power Generation Capacity, ____ yes, ____ no	
7	Alternative Heating / Cooking Capacity, ____ yes, ____ no	
8	Alternative Bug Out Location - Stocked, ____ yes, ____ no	
9	Land in a More Remote Area - Relocation, ____ yes, ____ no	
10	Are the grounds defined? , ____ yes, ____ no	
11	Are local area maps available? , ____ yes, ____ no	
12	Are sentry / watch locations established? , ____ yes, ____ no	
13	Are methods of relieving watches defined?, ____ yes, ____ no	
14	Are the 3 basic contingency plans developed / understood:	
	Recall system and requirements: ____ yes, ____ no	
	Relocation procedure: ____ yes, ____ no	
	Disbanding procedure: ____ yes, ____ no	
	Total:	
	Max Total:	

Item 1, consult a local area map or research populations of towns nearby to determine if any within 60 miles have a population of 50,000 or more. This can be determined by the symbol used for the town and comparing to the legend. If closer, divide distance to town by 60 and multiply by 4 to get points, if farther away than 60 miles enter 4 points.

Item 2, if the main shelter property has an underground bunker, enter 2 points, otherwise enter zero.

Item 3, if the property has a basement, enter 1 point, otherwise enter zero.

Item 4, if the property has a safe room, enter 1 point, otherwise enter zero.

Item 5, if there is a local sense of community where people will come to the aid of others, enter 2, if not enter zero.

Shelter Sustainability

Item 6, 7, and 8, if there exists the ability to generate power for shelter usage, an alternative heating and / or cooking capacity such as a wood stove, etc., or if things go from bad to worse to where the primary shelter must be abandoned, is there an alternative stocked bug out location, if yes enter 2 points each as applicable, if no enter zero.

Item 9, is there land in a more remote location to bug out to if the primary shelter must be abandoned (bug out) and is it stocked, if yes enter 2 points, if no enter zero.

Item 10, are the boundaries of the current shelter grounds or property defined and made known to those in the group, if yes enter 2 points, if no enter zero.

Item 11, are there local area maps available to plan excursions outside the shelter into the local area for recon or needed materials, if yes enter 2 points, if no enter zero.

Item 12 & 13, are sentry positions, watch locations, and shifts established, and are methods of relieving watch personnel established, if yes enter 2 points, if no enter zero.

Item 14, there are many types of contingency plans, but only three basic ones. Score 2 points each if they have been developed and are understood. There are potentially 32 points, adjust as needed for your situation.

Notes:

SAFETY / FIRST AID / MEDICAL

It is reasonable to believe someone will become injured through an accident, momentary carelessness, bad weather, or other external threat or event. Injuries may be minor to severe, but all present the risk of escalation into life threatening situations. Important is having established first aid kits for general and advanced treatment along with all adult team members receiving training in general first aid in order to treat injuries properly. When more severe injuries occur it is important to have at least a few adults trained in advanced first aid procedures and a methodology worked out to obtain external help when needed.

Sometimes doctors are not adverse to writing prescriptions for general or broad spectrum antibiotics when asked and informed of the reason for the request. If anyone is taking prescription medications on a regular basis it is important to stock at least 3 months or more ahead in case a long-term survival event happens as last minute supplies may not be available in time.

	Safety / First Aid / Medical	
		Points
1	Minimum of 1 fire extinguisher available in shelter	
2	3 month personal prescription medication supply	
3	Fire extinguisher in each vehicle	
4	General first aid kit	
5	Advanced first aid kit	
6	External source of first aid / medical help	
7	All adults trained in general first aid	
8	Minimum one-quarter adults trained in advanced first aid	
9	Availability of broad spectrum antibiotic(s)	
10	Other	
	Total:	
	Max Total:	18

General safety equipment is highly desirable and includes fire extinguishers both in the shelter and vehicles. Personal protective equipment is addressed under a separate area. The list in the preceding table is not meant to be all inclusive, but a starting point for thought to

SURVIVAL AUDIT & CALCULATIONS

adapt to your particular needs. Each area is fairly direct and self-explanatory. Each item scores 2 points if complied with and zero points if not. The total possible score is 18.

Notes:

TRANSPORTATION RESOURCES

While it is understood that there may be times and conditions where moving about any distance may require doing so on foot, it goes without saying the preferred method is by vehicle. This is especially true if forced to bug out and increases the likelihood of being able to take most if not all of your resources. Evaluation in the following table is made on the basis of maintaining motorized transportation.

	Transportation Resources		
		Count	Points
1	Total number of vehicles		
2	Total amount of vehicle fuel reserves		
3	Total fuel reserves needed based on 20 mi/gal		
4	Is there one or more 4-wheel drive vehicles? ___ yes, ___ no		
5	Are there any armored vehicles? ___ yes, ___ no		
6	Vehicles housed inside (not out in the open) ___ yes, ___ no		
Sustainability			
7	Are there alternative methods of transportation? ___ yes, ___ no		
8	Oil filters available		
9	Oil for oil changes available		
10	Oil filters needed		
11	Oil needed		
12	Number of spare tires available		
13	Spare tires needed based on 2 per vehicle		
14	Resources to repair a flat tire? ___ yes, ___ no		
15	Resources available to inflate a flat tire? ___ yes, ___ no		
16	Other		
		Total:	
		Max Total:	

Item 1, list the total number of vehicles at the shelter when all group members are present. Score 4 points if there is at least one vehicle or more per licensed adult driver, 2 points if between half and all adult licensed drivers, zero if less.

Item 2, list the amount of vehicle fuel reserves stored at the primary shelter location. A secondary location does not count because you are not there to utilize its resources. In addition, a combination of vehicles using gasoline and diesel complicates storage because additional space is required either underground or above ground and it may be more difficult to access multiple fuel stores in adverse, hostile conditions. Take into account these various factors if your vehicles utilize more than one type of fuel.

Item 3, multiply the number of vehicles in Item 1 by 300 and enter. This is the amount of fuel needed per vehicle to go 6,000 miles assuming a consumption of one gallon every 20 miles. Compare the amount on Item 2 to Item 2. If Item 3 is less than or equal to Item 2, enter 2 points. If Item 2 is half or more of Item 3, enter 1 point. If Item 2 is less than half of item 3, enter zero points.

Item 4, if there are one or more 4-whell drive vehicles per every 4 people (children included, example 8 people of which 4 are adults and 4 are children = 2 vehicles), score 2 points. Minimum is one vehicle for 4 people or less. A ratio of 6 people per 4-wheel drive vehicle, score 1 points, less score zero.

Item 5, if there are one or more armored vehicles, score 2 points, none score zero.

Item 6, if all vehicles are housed within a closed structure(s), score 2 points, half or more score 1 point, less than half score zero. Vehicles housed within buildings increase their security and hides guessing how large your group may be. It also reduces the chance of sheltering attackers and increases the odds that tires will not be shot out.

Transportation Sustainability

Item 7, are there alternative methods of transportation such as horses, horse or ox drawn cart or wagon, electric vehicles, etc. If yes inter 2 points, no zero points.

Item 8, how many oil filters per vehicle are available to perform oil changes for each vehicle based on 6,000 miles and changing every 3,000 miles. Oil and oil filters are important resources to maintain transportation in a survival and post survival scenario for many reasons.

Item 9, how many quarts of oil are available to perform oil changes for each vehicle based on 6,000 miles and changing every 3,000 miles. Different types of vehicles require different styles of filters, lubrication requirements, and quantities. Inventory your requirements prior to setting up materials.

Item 10, oil filter need is based upon changing filters with an oil change every 3,000 miles. Makes plans to stock materials for a minimum of 2 oil changes to include filters. Multiply the number of vehicles in Item 1 by 2, if Item 8 is equal to or larger than Item 10 score 2 points, if half as many score 1, less than half score zero.

Item 11 Oil Needed, multiply the amount of oil needed for an oil change in every vehicle as entered in Item 1 by 2. If the amount entered in Item 9 is greater than or equal to this amount score 2 points, greater than or equal to half score 1 point, less than half score zero.

Item 12 Spare Tires Available, count the spare tires available in stock for replacement on all vehicles entered in Item 1 and enter.

Item 13 Spare Tires Needed, based on the thought that bad conditions and hazards in a survival situation can damage tires beyond repair, the idea is to have at least 2 replacement tires of any type. Count the number of vehicles in Item 1 and multiply by 2. If Item 12 is greater than or equal to Item 13 enter 2 points, if half or more enter 1 point, less than half enter zero.

Item 14 Resources to Repair a Flat Tire, if there are materials available to repair punctures, etc in tires score 2 points, if not score zero.

Item 15 Resources to Inflate a Flat Tire, if there are resources to inflate flat tires i.e. pressurized air tank, hand pump, pressure gauge, etc. score 2 points, if not score zero points.

There are potentially 22 points, adjust as needed for your group's size.

Notes:

LEADERSHIP

The leadership area is by nature general and covers a broad range of topics with a few questions. It is intended to provoke thought on how the survival group functions, how leadership takes place, and interaction with the local community.

Leadership		
		Points
1	Is there an universally accepted leader?	
2	Regular team meetings?	
3	Local government participation?	
4	Local government monitoring?	
5	Monitoring of state and federal government?	
Sustainability		
6	Is there a second in command?	
7	Team understanding of the chain of command?	
8	Rules in place for enforcing team behavior?	
9	Rules in place for enforcing laws?	
10	Other	
	Total:	
	Max Total:	

Item 1 Universally Accepted Leader, this question is intended to explore how the group's leader came into being. Was choice of the leader because he / she owned the property for the survival location? Was the leader chosen by consensus? Was the leader self-appointed? Understanding how the leader came to fulfill this role is important in determining potential problems down the road when important life or death decisions may be made and how well they will be followed. If there is a universally accepted leader, score 2 points, if not score zero.

Item 2 Regular Scheduled Meetings, addresses review of preparedness status, updates on items that needed to be accomplished, and schedules of when drills may take place to practice how well everyone is organized in meeting expected duties. This serves as a key planning and review function with input from the entire group on all aspects of the survival functions. If these meeting are scheduled on regular basis, score 2 points, if not score zero.

Item 3 Local Government Participation, serves to monitor what is going on in local government and what actions plans are in place to be acted upon in case of a long-term survival event. This acts in keeping your "ear to the ground" and is important in knowing what actions local authorities may decide to take. It is possible that the local authorities may want to search and take any stocks of food and other supplies stored in private homes to be used for the "greater good" of everyone. It would be nice to know of these actions and how they plan to execute them beforehand so preparations can be made. This is also a good source of inside information on what is taking place outside the local area. Score 2 points if there is participation and zero if not.

Item 4 Local Government Monitoring, is keeping abreast of what is going on within local government and official agencies such as the sheriff and National Guard. This may be through monitoring radio communications, meeting attendance, etc. Score 2 points if this is done and zero if not.

Item 5 Monitoring State and Federal Government, keeping in touch with what is transpiring in the state and federal governments as far as relief actions, formal curfews, restrictions on travel, and confiscation or seizure of personal properties is of interest in preparing responses. This will primarily be through public postings as well as operating television, cable, and radio stations that may include emergency broadcasts. Score 2 points if there are means to monitor these broadcasts and / or keeping up with locally posted notices, zero points if not.

Leadership Sustainability

Item 6, a Recognized Second in Command, is necessary for dividing the responsibilities of running daily operations and having someone in charge of outside excursions for materials and supplies while someone maintains shelter security. Should the primary leader become incapacitated then there is someone recognized to step up. Score 2 points if there is a recognized second in command, zero if not.

Item 7, does the team understand the chain of command? This is necessary for an understanding of who is responsible for what and where limitations exist. These need defining ahead of time for many areas such as food distribution, setting watches, other resource allocations, etc. Score 2 points if this is in effect and zero if it is not in effect.

Item 8 involves an understanding of expected normal behavior for team members and what is expected if these norms are not followed. There are too many possibilities to cover here, but it is important to understand these to prevent surprises and undermine team cohesiveness. Score 2 points if there is an understanding of expected normal team behavior and zero if not.

Item 9 involves how laws will be enforced. This is important in that the rule of law and courts may not be in effect or reverted to martial law. If enforcement falls to the team, will guilt and punishment be decided by the team leader or a panel of team members. How will enforcement take place? Score 2 points if this is established as part of the team functions and zero if not. There are potentially 18 points.

Notes:

SKILLS TO TRADE

Skills and Items to Trade may involve a much wider range of skills and items than listed in this table. Almost any applied trade, knowledge for training or education, and items that someone needs makes these of value to those not possessing them. The table lists some common things that come easily to mind that would be of value in a long-term scenario.

Skills / Items to Trade		
	Skills Items	Points
1	Mechanical repair	
2	Gunsmithing	
3	Blacksmith	
4	Leather Working	
5	Sawmill	
6	Fire Wood Cutting	
7	Food preservation training	
8	Water purification	
9	Laundry items (detergent, bleech, etc.	
10	Toilet paper	
11	Maintenance materials	
12	Crops / Livestock	
13	Seeds	
14	Matches	
15	Razors	
16	Medications	
17	Nails	
18	Files	
19	Hair Cutting	
20	Animal slaughtering	
21	Other	
	Total:	
	Max Total:	

If the team or team members possess any of the items listed in the table score 2 points, if not applicable "N/A" score 2 points, if not score zero. This is a very flexible area with an additional line for "other" to add additional areas. In a post event world, having skills that are in demand and / or materials to barter puts an individual or group at an advantage. If other people know about the material possessions of a person or group, having material things that others may want increases the risk that attempts may be made to take them by force.

Two areas not included in the table are weapons and ammunition. This is because these are items that may be used against you or your group. Sometime after the survival event there may exist a time when you are familiar with and trust individuals in the surrounding community. It is a personal or team choice to trade in these areas based on trust, relationships, and whether or not the risk can be justified. Security many times trumps breathing, water, food, and eating because it ensures that breathing, water, and food are continued. This is potentially a long, detailed area, and it is up to the group to decide how to manage based on what is currently possessed and what future desires / requirements are believed to be.

Notes:

UNIQUE FACTORS

Unique factors is a special category that covers the unique things individuals or groups possess in skills, knowledge, materials, the physical environment, training, and so forth. This allows you or your group to inventory these special areas that are brought to a long-term survival situation that improves the odds and / or provides an edge in making it through difficult times.

Unique Factors	
	Points
1	
2	
3	
4	
5	
Sustainability	
6	
7	
8	
9	
10	
11	
12	
13	
14	
15	
Total:	
Max Total:	

As an open category, list all things that make your situation better adapted, more skillful, better situated, and so forth in meeting a long-term survival demand. Score 2 points for the areas listed that are not covered in other survey areas.

Unique Factors Sustainability

Because this is an open category and not possible to determine what items will be added to the Unique Factors table, it is also not possible to determine what specialized elements will be needed to sustain the Unique Factors in the long term. It is up to the individual or group to use their knowledge and imagination in determining what support in terms of replacements, consumables, and expendables are needed to administer or maintain these in working order.

Notes:

CLOTHING AND PERSONAL PROTECTIVE EQUIPMENT

This area addresses many of the personal items individuals and team members need to focus on for the long-term. While many of these items may seem obvious, they can easily be overlooked when focus is on such things as weapons, ammunition, food, water, and so forth. Items that wear out over time such as clothing need particular attention and this is of particular importance if there are growing children involved who will go through everything from shirts and pants to shoes.

	Clothing & Personal Protective Equipment	
		Points
1	Clothing suitable for cold weather – 2 sets minimum	
2	Clothing suitable for hot weather – 2 sets minimum	
3	Shoes suitable for outdoor work i.e. boots, etc.	
4	Earth tone / camouflage clothing blending in with surroundings	
5	Head gear, gloves, etc. for manual labor	
6	Everyone a suitable backpack for bugging out	
7	Everyone a suitable knife for daily usage	
8	Everyone a suitable portable water supply method	
9	Pre-arranged travel paths, locations, etc.	
10	Body armor for armed attack	
11	Gas masks, filters, and replacement filter	
12	Plan (list) in place on what to pack	
13	Sewing kit for repairs	
14	Other	
	Total:	
	Max Total:	

Many of the items listed here are self-explanatory, but here are a few comments about some entries. There is always the possibility, however remote, that things will go from bad to truly ugly and there will be a need to exit the shelter on foot. Good planning requires addressing having everyone a suitable backpack, some method of hydration if only a canteen, and a written practiced plan in place on who takes what. One of the most simple and useful tools that separate people from animals is a knife. Everyone needs a fixed blade knife, preferably with a full tang for strength as well as a folding knife. There is also a need for body armor and gas masks while at the shelter in case of an armed attack as one cannot negate the possibility of people using police or military ordinance against the group.

There is a need for a plan and / or listing of mandatory and optional items to pack in case the bug out scenario is executed. It goes almost without saying that food, weapons, methods of fire starting, planned evacuation routes, etc. are included in these preparations. In a high stress, time critical situation of bugging out, it is best to have these backpacks prepared ahead of time with the packing requirements checked and cross checked to be as ready as possible to avoid forgetting essential items at the last instant.

Score 2 points for each item or if not applicable, zero if needed but not included. The current table allows for a total of 26 total points. Add additional items and areas as your particular situation requires.

Notes:

HYGIENE MAINTENANCE

Hygiene maintenance is an area frequently overlooked in planning for a survival scenario. Experience from just weekend camping trips are frequent reminders of the possibility of leaving without a toothbrush or paste, forgetting the salt or pepper, and so on. Hygiene is important in long-term survival situations because of the possibility of living in limited space (especially if in a bunker) and as anyone with submarine or close quarter living experience such as a military barracks will tell you, illness and disease can spread rapidly in close quarters environments. If you have school age children you know by experience that when one child gets sick in the classroom, most of them also get sick as well as bringing it home to share with everyone there.

	Hygiene Maintenance	
		Points
1	6 bars of soap per person	
2	Ability to bathe daily	
3	Ability to do personal laundry weekly	
4	Ability to launder bedding weekly	
5	Insect repellent	
6	Tooth paste (6) per person + toothbrush	
7	Female hygiene products as needed	
Sustainability		
8	Ability to dispose of trash properly	
9	Ability to dispose of household water	
10	Internment of human remains	
11	Other	
12	Other	
	Total:	
	Max Total:	

The requirements for soap and toothpaste are based on an inability to obtain these during the 270-day period and represent minimums. Dentists may be few and far between and staving off the need for their services is important. Cleaning clothing and bedding on a scheduled basis reduces stress in having to put up with bad odors and reduces a dirty environment. The same goes for having the ability to bathe daily. Insect repellent is not a necessity, but makes the task of standing watch outside more tolerable if mosquitoes the size of house cats are not trying to feed on you. It is also important to realize the unique hygiene requirements of women and prepare supplies based on their inputs.

Hygiene Maintenance Sustainability

When considering sanitation requirements, a method of trash disposal is important. Recycling can be very useful, but some things need burial or burning to prevent attracting flies, rodents, etc. that can carry disease. Waste water and solid waste disposal is also important for the same reasons and prevents breeding areas for mosquitoes and other problem pests.

Important is the realization and preparation for the internment of human remains. If under armed attack, it is conceivable that some of those attacking will die and their group will abandon them where they fall, leaving them to the devices of Mother Nature. Realistically, it is also possible that team members will die in defense of or on excursions outside the shelter. However gruesome, there needs to be a plan in place to bury these individuals to prevent disease and other pestilence while maintaining security.

Score 2 points for each area, zero if not prepared. Add additional categories as needed and adjust point totals. The current table allows for a minimum of 20 points.

Notes:

SHELTER MAINTENANCE

This is an additional area where there seems little attention in survival situations. Remember this is not just for the weekend, but meant to last 9 months or longer. Maintaining a close living environment requires constant vigilance in keeping everything in order and monitoring resource consumption.

	Shelter Maintenance	
		Points
1	Daily cleaning	
2	Maintaining orderly existence, no clutter	
3	Updating inventory of on-hand items	
4	Evaluation of system functions i.e. water, sanitation, etc.	
5	Security systems	
Sustainability		
6	Air / Water / other filters	
7	Repair of broken window(s)	
8	Repair of damaged door(s)	
9	Full / temporary repair of roof damage	
10	Repair of damaged wall(s)	
11	Repair of damaged outbuildings	
12	Spare light bulbs, fluorescent tubes, etc.	
13	Other	
	Total:	
	Max Total:	

It goes without saying that everyone must help in maintaining the living areas in a clean, neat, and orderly manner. This responsibility should not fall on a single individual and the leader needs to insure that one person does not become the maid for all team members.

Shelter Maintenance Sustainability

Many things may happen over the long-term survival period. Storms can be more devastating than attacks from refugees and gangs. There is a need to have in place the ability to replace various water and air filters, repair broken windows, and repair damaged doors, walls, and outbuildings. Some shelter items also have life cycles and include not only filters, but light bulbs, fluorescent light tubes, candles, and oil lamp wicks to name a few. Planning

SURVIVAL AUDIT & CALCULATIONS

ahead for periodic replacement of these items as well as repair of damage can improve security and the quality of living in the long run.

Score 2 points for each item in this table and add or delete items as fitting to your situation and needs. Current table allows for 24 points.

Notes:

AUXILIARY EQUIPMENT

Auxiliary equipment enables many everyday jobs to be accomplished more efficiently and with less physical labor. The more equipment that is available to meet survival requirements the greater the possibility of providing materials or services to others in the community in trade for their goods and services.

	Auxiliary Equipment	
		Points
1	Fuel i.e. gasoline, diesel	
2	Oil	
3	Farm equipment i.e. tractor, backhoe, etc.	
4	Chain saw	
5	Generator	
	Sustainability	
6	Spare parts; spark plugs, belts, etc	
7	Grinder, files, etc. to sharpen equipment	
8	Hoes, rakes, pitch fork, etc. for cultivation	
9	Baskets, tubs, boxes, etc. for harvesting	
10	Spare parts for plumbing, irrigation, toilets	
11	Breaking & entering equipment	
12	Axe	
13	Shovels and other digging equipment	
14	Other	
15	Other	
	Total:	
	Max Total:	

Fuel and Oil, Items 1 & 2 may be different than that needed for vehicles in that a different grade is required and oil may be required as a fuel additive for equipment to function properly, i.e. a chainsaw.

Items 3, 4, & 5 are self explanatory in providing needed support to the group in several important areas such as ground preparation for planting crops, harvesting trees for lumber and firewood in the summer months, and providing electrical power for a number of electrical devices from refrigeration to shop equipment. Key in these areas is the broad application of a few pieces of equipment that make a large impact on quality and sustainability of life.

Auxiliary Equipment Sustainability

Under Sustainability the items listed are general in nature with the possibility of adding many others. To make an extensive list is not practical as many items could be left out or added depending upon the viewpoint and scenario envisioned. It is important to realize that there may be a need to have tools for breaking and entering buildings and secured areas in order to acquired needed materials and supplies from facilities no longer in operation. Such situations may present high risk due to others having previously taken over these facilities or arriving at the same time with equal goals in mind. This may require dividing the spoils and will always require careful planning ahead of time.

Score 2 points for each item listed and those added to this list. Score zero points if needed, but not available. If not applicable to your situation, N/A, score 2 points. The current table allows for a minimum of 26 points.

Notes:

ABILITY TO TRAIN / EDUCATE OTHER PEOPLE

In a major, long-term survival situation, especially one where preparations are made for a breakdown in the social-economic structure, it may take years or decades before life returns to a resemblance of normalcy. People with education and technical skills need to pass this learning and training on to the next generation. Those who will advance and better their position in life after such a major event will be individuals who are better educated and trained than anyone making an existence at a subsistence level.

Many of the materials and devices i.e. weapons, generators, filtering systems, and building methods for homes and infrastructure came from people who understood mathematics, engineering, and other applied sciences. The materials and knowledge passed on to the next generations cannot be overestimated in value contributed for increased and sustained prosperity.

Ability to Train / Educate People		
		Points
1	Ability to educate children	
2	Ability to educate in technical / trades	
3	Ability to train in survival skills	
4	Redundant / cross train division of labor	
5	Other	
	Total:	
	Max Total:	

Ability to Train and Educate takes the long view, not the short-term, and may prove critical to sustained survival in the upcoming generations. Item 1 and 2, Ability to Educate Children and Ability to Educate in Technical Skills / Trades, may prove one of the most difficult challenges in both a survival and post-survival world. Many of the people with professional and technical education and training may be few and far between i.e. doctors, dentists, bridge designers, and so forth. It is conceivable that entire trades and professions will become extinct, at least in the short-term. The immediate need will be for broad knowledge in multiple related fields. Facilities may be nonexistent. Materials such as books, paper, calculators, computers, and other materials and supplies may be in short supply if available at all. Possessing these skills and / or materials may prove very lucrative as there will be great need.

The ability to train others in survival skills has an immediate and long lasting impact on people surviving a major long-term event. There also exists a need to cross train people to perform multiple functions and jobs in creating a broader division of labor in case someone is busy doing another job or becomes incapacitated due to illness or injury.

Because of its forward looking nature to educate children in the technical and trade professions, score 8 points for each if this ability exists, zero if not for Items 1 & 2. Training others in survival skills and cross training for various jobs provides a skill that can provide a commodity for trade and increases one's personal value for long-term because other people will provide greater security and protection to such a valuable resource. Score 8 points for each if this ability exists, zero if not. Total table points are 32, adjust as your situation varies.

Notes:

WORSHIP / SPIRITUAL

Faith in God by whatever Name can provide a source of strength and peace in the highly stressful and unpredictable environment of long-term survival. Many people experience a need for faith of some kind or renewal of beliefs during events where there is great risk such as combat or personal peril. It goes without saying that this is an area of personal choice.

Worship / Spiritual		
		Points
1	Designated worship leader	
2	Bibles or similar worship materials	
3	Hymnals, etc	
4	Christian and other worship music DCs	
5	Other	
6	Other	
	Total:	
	Max Total:	

Score 2 points for each area and zero if it does not apply. This is an optional area not added into the overall point score, but acts as bonus points. The current table allows a minimum of 8 points.

Notes:

Summary

The following table lists all audit elements, the table page, and columns for points on your score. As a summary, list the modifications you made to the possible points score and points you or your group achieved in each area to provide an overall picture on the entire audit. Some areas are more critical than others and it is a personal or group decision on how to approach and prioritize these. Scores below 95% in any one area should be considered a deficiency and receive additional attention.

Summary Table			
Element	Page	Points	Score
Specialized Scenarios			
Nuclear	1		
Biological	2		
Chemical	3		
People	6		
Water Reserves	8		
Food Reserves	11		
Communications	13		
Security			
Defense and Assault Rifles	16		
Hunting / Sniping Rifles	18		
Defensive Handguns	19		
Defensive / Hunting Shotguns	21		
Small Game / Varmint Weapons	22		
Ammunition Reloading	24		
Shelter Resources	26		
Safety / First Aid / Medical	28		
Transportation Resources	30		
Leadership	33		
Skills to Trade	36		
Unique Factors	38		
Clothing and PPE	40		
Hygiene Maintenance	42		
Shelter Maintenance	44		
Auxiliary Equipment	46		
Ability to Train / Educate	48		
Worship / Spiritual	50		
	Total:		

ABOUT THE AUTHOR

Joseph Bounds served in the enlisted ranks of the United States Air Force and earned his bachelor's degree while on active duty with the Strategic Air Command. After commissioning, he served as a Maintenance Officer on the B-1B Bomber Test Team at Edwards Air Force Base, California where as a junior officer he was assigned the additional duty of nuclear fallout shelter commander during the Cold War. Since leaving the service, he has earned a master degree in Quality Assurance from California State University, Carson, California and certification by the American Society for Quality as a Six Sigma Black Belt. He has lead numerous internal audit teams, created layered audits, and taught the principles of continuous improvement with businesses and at the college level. A personal goal was to earn his doctorate degree which he accomplished in Business Administration / Management at Argosy University, graduating in 2012 on the Atlanta, Georgia campus. Dr. Bounds is author of two additional publications: *Executive Greed* which is based on his doctoral research into establishing executive compensation metrics and, *PSR Mars* a science fiction novel. He brings skills learned in auditing, management and six sigma improvement techniques to creating this audit manual for long-term survival preparations.

www.ingramcontent.com/pod-product-compliance
Lightning Source LLC
Chambersburg PA
CBHW081857170526
45167CB00007B/3048